Claiming Kindred

Previous poetry collections by D. M. Black

With Decorum (Scorpion Press), 1967
Penguin Modern Poets 11 (with Peter Redgrove and
D. M. Thomas), 1968
The Educators (Barrie & Rockliff / Cresset Press), 1969
The Happy Crow (M. Macdonald), 1974
Gravitations (M. Macdonald), 1979
Collected Poems, 1964-1987 (Polygon), 1991
Love as Landscape Painter (translations from Goethe)
(Fras Publications), 2006

D.M. BLACK
Claiming Kindred

PUBLICATIONS
2011

Published by Arc Publications
Nanholme Mill, Shaw Wood Road
Todmorden OL14 6DA, UK
www.arcpublications.co.uk

Design by Tony Ward
Printed in Great Britain by the
MPG Book Group, Bodmin & King's Lynn

978 1906570 46 0 pbk
978 1906570 47 7 hbk

ACKNOWLEDGEMENTS:

The author would like to thank the editors of the following magazines and anthologies in which earlier versions of these poems appeared: *Chapman, The Dark Horse, Fras, Modern Poetry in Translation, Painted / Spoken, Poetry London, Soundings, Southfields, The Swansea Review, Thumbscrew, Verse; A Quark for Mister Mark: 101 Poems about Science,* ed. M. Riordan and J. Turney (Faber, 2000), *Emergency Kit,* ed. J. Shapcott and M. Sweeney (Faber, 1996), *Faber Book of Twentieth Century Scottish Poetry,* ed. D. Dunn (Faber, 1992), *Generations,* ed. M. Hart and J. Loader (Penguin, 1998), *Best Scottish Poems 2004,* ed. H. Whyte (Scottish Poetry Library Online), *Wild Reckoning,* ed. M. Riordan and J. Burnside (Calouste Gulbenkian Foundation, 2004), also the Brindin Press translations website, edited by Brian Cole.

The author is also grateful to many individuals who have commented creatively on these poems, and in particular to Robert Chandler, Elizabeth Cook and Martha Kapos. This group has at different times included Robin Leanse, Christopher Reid and Carole Satyamurti, and has now met regularly for some twenty years, in friendship and to discuss their writing. His debt to it, and to them, is incalculable.

Cover picture: 'Strathmiglo' by John McLean from
the private collection of Ian Collins.

Supported by
**ARTS COUNCIL
ENGLAND**

Editor for the UK and Ireland: John W. Clarke

…something in us like the catbird's song…
That, harsh or sweet, and of its own accord,
Proclaims its many kin.

RICHARD WILBUR

Mon âme, grande fille, vous aviez vos façons qui
ne sont pas les nôtres.

ST-JOHN PERSE

CONTENTS

I

Voices for children

Natives of poverty, children of malheur,
The gaiety of language is our seigneur.

WALLACE STEVENS

KEW GARDENS
i.m. Ian Armstrong Black, 1902-1971

Distinguished scientist, to whom I greatly defer
(Old man, moreover, whom I dearly love),
I walk today in Kew Gardens, in sunlight the colour of honey
Which flows from the cold autumnal blue of the heavens to
      light these tans and golds,
These ripe corn and leather and sunset colours of the East
      Asian liriodendrons,
Of the beeches and maples and plum-trees and the stubborn
      green banks of the holly-hedges –
And you walk always beside me, you with your knowledge
      of names
And your clairvoyant gaze, in what for me is sheer panorama
Seeing the net or web of connectedness. But today it is I who speak
(And you are long dead, but it is to you I say it):

'The leaves are green in summer because of chlorophyll
And the flowers are bright to lure the pollinators,
And without remainder (so you have often told me)
These marvellous things that shock the heart the head can
      account for;
But I want to sing an excess which is not so simply explainable,
To say that the beauty of the autumn is a redundant beauty,
That the sky had no need to be this particular shade of blue,
Nor the maple to die in flames of this particular yellow,
Nor the heart to respond with an ecstasy that does not beget
      children.
I want to say that I do not believe your science
Although I believe every word of it, and intend to understand it;
That although I rate that unwavering gaze higher than almost
      everything,

There is another sense, a hearing, to which I more deeply attend.
Thus I withstand and contradict you, I, your child,
Who have inherited from you the passion which causes me to
   oppose you.'

FOR AND AGAINST THE ENVIRONMENT

I have come out to smell the hyacinths which again in this North
     London garden
Have performed a wonderful feat of chemistry and hauled that
     delectable perfume
Out of the blackish confection of clay and potsherds which feebly
     responds when I name it *flower-bed*;
And so wet was the Spring that I clipped the grass with shears,
     to prevent the mower sliding in mud
And my attempt to dig the beds to enhance their fertility
     foundered, caked with clods.
But today the April sun blazes from a cloudless sky, and the
     lawn, drenched with raindrops
Like an utterly saturated sponge has unfurled and surrendered
     its freight,
And – where do they come from? – the small pert insects emerge
     onto the skin of dryness
Like Noah's prospecting pigeon and at once they are up to all
     sorts of business,
And the buds you had thought paralyzed if not embalmed are
     surely discernibly plumper
And purpler or pinker than you remember them yesterday, and
     the hum of potential life
Swells with its distinctive excitement to just short of the
     threshold of actual audibility
Through which it bursts, perhaps, by way of the throat of that
     unceasing ingenious blackbird
Poised on my neighbour's gutter against the blue of the sky. O,
     wonderful world!
And here are two absolute flowers, new as babies:

They have bowed their heads for weeks in their bashful, fleecy
    pods,
But today they stare up at me bravely, giving all they have got
And making at last no pretence they are anything else but
    anemones
And this is their hour, and if they don't impress now they will
    never impress,
But they do, and to support my judgment a small fly is clambering
    deliberately over the organ stops of their stamens
Making, I do not doubt, marvellous music. O, wonderful world!
And the ant is rushing at immense speed over the lifeless plains
    of the rose-bed
Which are not plains to her but ridged and crested with salts
    and terrible canyons,
And she winds every which way through them but never
    forgets her sense of direction
For she is not such a fool as to think, but attends to the sun
    and the earth's magnetism,
And I am shocked by my own thought, that my own thought
May be a blind lobe on the body of the great creature of Evolution,
An experiment which does not carry the future. And meanwhile
    here is this ant,
Only the most distant relation of Mozart and Shakespeare, yet
    unmistakably designed for survival,
Nosing about through the clods like an exceptionally fleet piece of
    earth-moving equipment
And not in the least reciprocating the warm concern she has
    evoked in me,
And the same is true of the blackbird, whose song I salute, and

the anemone
Whose sleek pods I have fondled, and the clods which I have
  rendered more fertile,
And at this moment, speaking now as one of the Lords of Creation,
Speaking as one of the Shepherds of Being, unique bearers of
  conscious and self-conscious life,
I have to declare my preference within all the sparkling welter
(O, wonderful world!) and I do, keeping the ant firmly fixed in
  my gaze:
Great and more fragile is man than ant or earth or anemone
And in or out of the glass-house of Nature, let him above all not
  be seduced.

APUS APUS

Cupid's bow, black devil, pre-Christian,
motor-bike rider coming at us over the roof-tops –
always in a crowd, scattering
to the four dimensions, exultant, shouting –

who shun the solid world, footless, feed
on wind-carried particles, mate in the air, three years at a stretch
remain aloft. Born
under these gentle English eaves, but more truly

native of a savager landscape, Africa, screeching, tumultuous,
no songbird. You voice the leonine heat,
concentrate in a mad crescent the black blue of summer,
go wild, pretending fear, before the storm-cloud. Acrobat,
kami-kaze, too shrewd to really die –

All night, drifting insomniac a mile above us,
you long for dawn to shatter the horizon!

THE BUMBLE BEE

I went into a room I had neglected.
He or she was crawling torpidly against the doorstep
inside my tall glass door which opens onto the balcony.
Outside was a high blue day in wonderful dizzy midsummer.
I thought: he has been here for days, is starving and close to death.
But I invited him to step onto a compliments slip from the
    British Journal of Psychiatry,
and languidly, like a child with flu, he consented – one leg, two,
    and then, with my shove, the whole of his body –
I opened the door and laid the freighted compliments slip on
    the earth of a window-box.
I thought: let him die at least in sight of the sun and the chestnut-
    trees, the extravagant summer roses.
He lay still. I turned to go in
but a sizzling arrested me –
I looked back – he was gone – Like a humming arrow
I saw him sing into the green depths of the air, then higher and
    higher
on a swerving, all-but straight path, lofting superbly above
    the tree-tops
like someone in no doubt at all where he's got to get to.

IN PRAISE OF RECONNECTING

When I was a boy in Lushoto school, Tanganyika,
playing marbles with Robin and Henry, one marble bounced in
      the dust
and sprang off down a steep bank of scrubby grasses.
It was gone at once. The sun-hot air
carried no memory and no trace of its passing.
We stood and looked helplessly down the almost vertical slope.
Nothing but shrivelled grass and dust, and the occasional ant,
      the occasional fly...
And we would have given up, shrugging our shoulders,
had not Patrick the brother of Henry said: *let's set*
another marble to find it, put
another marble where you last saw the lost one –
and Henry picked up a shiny blue marble
from our small supply
and held it between two grass tussocks at the crest of the slope
and let go. It vanished at once among the dusty grass-stems –
and nothing happened a moment –
and the moment grew longer –
and then, from the grass far down on the bank, there came
a quiet, unostentatious *clink*
I have heard for six decades.

MR. GREENWAY'S INSTRUCTIONS

When you're feeding a lion, boy, feeding a lion,
You don't just put out the pot,
As if you were feeding the cat!
You bang it down with a clang of iron,
Bang it again with a clang of iron,
And a crash like a pistol-shot!
The lion will hunger at that, boy,
Lions get hungry at that.

When I was a kid, and less than a kid, and still in the womb of
    my mother,
Millions of men all over the earth began to murder each other,
Poles and Danes and people in planes and people on all the seas,
Gypsies and blind and gaily inclined and Jews and Japanese;
And I was a kid, and less than a kid, and still in the waters of mystery,
But, Daddy, you were a man, you had to play your part in history.
Daddy, I guess you had to prove you were a hell of a fellow,
A true-blue Brit with pluck and grit and not a hint of yellow –
But whatever the truth you'd missed some youthful need to be
    centre-stage,
And now war's advance gave a second chance to that ebullient rage.
You marched away for a year and a day to fight the frightful Gerry,
But I was a kid like all other kids, and I couldn't stay in a belly;
And I shouldn't say *a year and a day,* for I mock my mother's tears:
You left her alone and far from her home for four appalling years.
She did her best from pillar to post in lodgings and cheap hotels,
With two young children under her feet and small help from
    anyone else.
As for the care folk had to spare I doubt it could have been littler,
For this was in racist South Africa, and the Boers were rooting
    for Hitler.
She did her best – but was governed by restlessness and
    tremendous grief,
And fear as well (and fury as well), and no-one to bring relief.
What did she do in the Little Karoo? what did she do at the Cape?
What did she do up in Malmesbury, or in Ceres, home of the grape?
How did she live? who did she love? History has no reply.
When I think of her lot like a bee in a bottle she could neither
    settle nor fly.

Daddy, I guess you would never suspect the havoc your
    soldiering made,
Not in the breast of the enemy, but where your children played,
Not where Hitler and Himmler put their murderous plans in train,
But in the heart of a woman whose love snapped from too long
    a strain.
Then peace returned, and you returned, to what you thought
    would be peace,
And found yourself banned in a no-man's-land where the
    sniping never ceased.
What peace restored were the endless wars of hurt and
    incomprehension,
In which combat zone for devotion shown I give you honourable
    mention.

MOMBASA, 1948

Not that I have created God himself!
not that I have created the universe! –
but that without me it would all be utterly different
and without you it would all be unimaginable.
This brain smaller than a coconut
gives light to the world,
lights up this enormous sky, this flashing sea, the blue mirrors of
    the blue-gum leaves and the waving green of the palm-fronds,
and thanks to you, dear friend, dear remembered friend,
I distinguish leaf from twig, and twig from branch,
recognise bulbul and hornbill, know the rough heavy fruit of
    the breadfruit tree,
and carve my own name on the shining white of the sand.
Were it not for me, were it not for you
there would be millions of worlds, very possibly, indeed very
    probably, wonderful
but not this, my only world, with its great gulf of air and sunlight
which I breathe as deeply and rapturously as a thirsty baby put
    to the breast,
not this sun and not this interminably changing ocean
sparkling, and blue, and living, speaking to me with every tint
    and facet
– this world I eat, so great is my love and delight in it!

Not that I have created God himself,
not that I have created the universe:
it is there before me, utterly substantial,

in no way dependent on my perceiving it,
in no way at all remotely resembling a dream.
It is there in its absolute clarity utterly mysterious,
and I praise it, beyond expression, praise it
beyond expression, and my love is the only thing in me
that, like the flying fish, leaps and transcends
– leaps and may hope to answer in kind this marvellous reality.

II

Omens of death

The purpose of poetry is to remind us
how difficult it is to remain just one person,
for our house is open, there are no keys in the doors,
and invisible guests come in and out at will.

CZESLAW MILOSZ

PENCIL SKETCHES

1. *The philosopher*

Being is not a predicate, he said.
I'm unpersuaded. Maybe Homer's dead
Who fought and shoved to lap the steaming blood
Knew something Kant never quite understood.

2. *Portrait of a woman*

Time she let her father join the drifting shades –
But she can't do it! Each nuance,
Each folded harmonic of male authority,
Spins her back half a century to where, once
On a sunlit lawn amid the gardening tools,
Poisoned with hatred, a small girl spat defiance.

3. *The one described as "slightly gaga"*

He watched those vile regimes expire
In thunderstorms of blood and fire
But did not hate them as he ought.
As millions died, he only thought
How soft the white clouds on the breeze,
How motherly the swaying trees.

4. *The one who couldn't cry*

A virtuous man, he paid his way:
And no one ever heard him say
Things more impetuous than he meant –
So thriftily from day to day
He watched how joy and longing lay,
And kept his loves ambivalent.

5. *She recognises the limits of individual achievement*

She tips the curdled milk into the drain.
But does that mean the cow has lived in vain?
She will not think of anything so scary.
The cattle not the cow supply the dairy.

6. *The seducer*

How sweet the smile of the practised seducer!
It warms your heart. You could love those melting eyes!
Yet notice how different he is when he meets an accuser:
Like a rat in a trap he snarls, and lies, and lies.

7. *She who was always humble*

If she can subdue her soul
Maybe God's thunder will not roll.
Maybe the lightnings, poised to strike,
Will go away, behind her back,
And God will swathe her with his love
If she crouches low enough.

8. *A kindly, elderly couple*

She told him to shut up! shut up!! shut up!!!
She wouldn't hear it!!! Thwarted, he complied.
Winter filled up the ancient pine-forest;
Snow covered motorway and mountainside.

9. *The prince who was a frog*

The Prince who was a frog
Until the Princess kissed him
Fears with every kiss
Froghood will reinvest him.

Therefore, lively girls,
Who kiss, and want to play,
Be careful with your Prince
Who may yet spring away.

10. *Colleague*

Pumps your hand – "how good to see you!" –
Warming smile and wandering eye –
Like a wave he washes through you,
Lifts you up, and lets you dry.

A COUPLE IN COIGACH

She didn't want to be running after some encounter with God!
She wanted an expectable orderliness, faces around the breakfast
        table,
The daily doing and planning, the planting of montbretias and
        cyclamen,
The worrying about school and school-friends, the delight in quite
        ordinary achievements.
She didn't want to be running after some encounter with
        greatness!
She loved the colour of the indigo lochs and the changing greens
        and greys and purples
In the walls of the valley, and the way birch-trees grow out of
        moss-covered rock.
She wanted nothing more than summer and winter, sunlight
        and gales,
In a world of which she was part, and with which she was
        fully engaged,
And from which she would in due time depart, sad to leave the
        round-dance of the seasons,
Still in love with her family and those great ever-altering rooms
        of skies and islands.

Whereas he –
It was he who was, O, always aspiring, to whom the visible world
Was a rind on something profounder, the shore-line
Of a huge continent yet unpenetrated. Who hungered after love
Beyond these touchings and smilings, these age-marked hands
        and bodies.
He wanted it all to matter: to record the outcome of his meditation,

To say: these were his findings. He wanted to be remembered
In a great memory, like the sky, and he was unhappy
With the transience of everything. He couldn't stop reflecting
How even the mountains, even Suilven,
Would not tomorrow have the same Gestalt as today, and yet
would have no awareness of their loss.
– How could he find satisfaction in her? How could he love
What could die and leave him to remember? He clung to himself,
he clung to something
Obscure, essential, like the shipwrecked non-swimmer
Clutching the seaweed-clad rock, seeing evidence everywhere
Of the tide's rising, and denying it.

THE MISTLETOE

She got him to make love behind a hedge,
Insisting recklessly they should both be naked.
She urged him with: *"you're man enough to take it!*
If someone comes, and wants to stare," she said,
"That's their problem!"

                  And so they did,
These middle-aged lovers, under a summer sky,
The traffic switching past unconsciously:
Each claimed a youth whose loss their skin conceded.

She seemed delighted; he was angry. Why
Should middle-age not challenge, eye to eye,
Its feared defeat? He walked across, to where

In a dry apple-tree, lichen-wrapped, half-dead,
Green flames of mistletoe blossomed overhead –
And wrenched that green bush off, and flung it clear.

THE YOUNG WOMAN DOCTOR

for Edgar Nelson Smith

When the rather beautiful young woman doctor
Said, "Can we have a word in private?" –
Then told you you had an inoperable cancer,
Even then you wanted to flirt with her, wanted
To touch that firm hand, further off than Mercury,
To bring a smile to those unstopping, talkative lips.
Your life revised itself. What you had thought
Provisional, those preludes to your greatness,
Now were the thing itself; that half-seen cloud
Resolved, became a solid mountain-range,
All earth you will have known. What rubbish dropped away,
Oceans you might have seen, children you might have fathered,
Extravagant soaring dreams of influence –
The kisses that you'd like to give this doctor
To drown that noble face in playfulness...
She stands, and holds her hand out. You are polite,
Of course, and take it. It is live and warm.
How the miscarrying baby clasps the umbilicus! –
All strength, all warmth, all goodness in that grasp.
You say: "Thank you, for speaking so directly."

TWO SHOTS AT AN ELEGY
i.m. Peter Caddy, 1917-1994

I

And news is brought, old man, of your death in a car-crash.
Age 76, in your fifth marriage,
It's impossible to imagine that deep chest,
Those commanding eyes, grown vague and impotent.
I loved you for your force, when you were younger.
I remember once – someone had been berated
For some sexual misdemeanour – all you said was:
"I've done it every way", and refused hypocrisy.
Rock-solid, healthy, with the good looks of a paratrooper,
You drove with accuracy and at compelling speed.
You always said you had an angel on the bonnet.
Maybe you did. I hope he killed you quickly.
Dear Peter, man of action, life-enhancer,
When you review your stay on earth with the assessors,
You'll send a jolt of adrenalin through all the waiting angels.

II

And news is brought, old man, of your death in a car-crash.
In youth you led climbers on Everest;
Later, aspiring higher,
You stood on a rock and thundered: "I AM POWER!!",
Not without reason. Always decisive, always in action,
You let women shape that great explosion of energy
You knew yourself to be. You said of Eileen:

She was the Love, your task to be the Light –
You put things over-simply, always. You
Gave house-room to such rubbish – flying saucers,
Channelled messages, menders of psychic envelopes,
Jewels brought down from Solomon himself… – And yet
If, as they say, our beliefs are what we act on,
One has to pack somehow the furnace walls
In which one's blaze can concentrate. –

How you loved action! how you loved it when
I said to you "How're things?" and you could look
Me level in the eye and answer: *"Humming!"* You
Were left proud, and I exhilarated
As if I had met Dick Turpin and his pistols! – Rubbish or not…
You changed more lives than most of us, Peter,
And most by increase of courage. I see a child
When I look more searchingly into that forceful gaze,
Turned from some pain with blazing blue defiance:
"No need for anyone, Mother, you've got *me!*" –
Mother's wonderful son, who chose the far horizon.

– And should I guess he chose his own death, finally?
A runaway van careened across the highway,
But I hear your light voice telling how life always,
Taken full volley, comes "in perfect timing".

THIRTEEN WAYS OF LOOKING AT BIRMINGHAM

1.

Imagine being poor bloody Jerusalem,
Unsmilingly screwed by three inexhaustible lovers.
Wouldn't it be much better to be Birmingham,
Over-rated by nobody?

2.

In the centre of Birmingham there is a square in which there is
    no traffic,
Presided over by a huge naked woman from whose hands flows
    water continually,
And the inhabitants of Birmingham walk up and down, or stand
    very still pretending to be statues of policemen,
Or they march about grinning and banging tambourines and
    chanting Hare Rama.
The inhabitants of Birmingham look rather prosperous without
    being at all ostentatious
And its young women smile unexpectedly as they pass pensive
    poets.
Well, Jerusalem is what it is, I dare say, and no doubt the same
    was true of Alexandria,
And Nineveh had a big reputation once though its ultimate
    fate was deplorable,
But let no-one say anything in disparagement of Birmingham
Birmingham thou art the flower of cities all.

3.

My mother's mother was the butcher's daughter
My mother's father was a shoemaker.
Those large families, in flat Northamptonshire,
Put out runners and tendrils all across the Midlands:
Alice, Nellie, Frank, Jack, Percy…
– Only my mother like the albatross
Crossed the great water, left behind
Those unmet cousins.
Sometimes I brush past them, I think,
Strolling through Birmingham.

4.

I split this gawky and rejected house-plant,
Sprawling unwatered on a shadowed counter,
Into three stems for propagation.
Each has grown bright, furred with emphatic quills,
Whorling out new leaves that open like the mouths of green and
        purple trumpets,
Fountaining out over the top in a fuss of violet purses.
And I learn from this plant something I have also learned from
        Birmingham:
The gallant assertion of life
The refusal to be made afraid by past experience.

5.

If you were the Minister for Haircuts,
How hard it would be to keep the nation's hair cut!
You would require a whole uniformed police-force equipped
        with towels and clippers,
Informers, on-the-spot fines, and summary powers of execution,
Costing a disturbing proportion of the Gross Domestic Product:
Even then you would do the job ineffectively.
Individual self-esteem is the answer,
Then each head of hair has its own highly motivated custodian.
– It's thoughts like this one sometimes has in Birmingham:
They have a sort of tolerance, a sort of humour

6.

I once knew a high-flier: her wish was to fly over Las Vegas
And look down on millions and millions of dollars.
It's curious to hear of a wish and be in no way tempted to share it –
I prefer my dollars face to face, and to keep my feet on the ground.
And she might have felt the same
If she had come from Birmingham.

7.

I gets weary, sang Paul Robeson,
An' sick of tryin'
An' tired of livin'
An' skeered of dyin'.–
I'm not a fool,
I know what he means,
And yet even in Birmingham
You can't just go rollin' along.

8.

The other day in the town of Jasper, Texas,
They tied a black man to the back of a pick-up
And dragged him along the roadway
Until at last his head came apart from his body
And bounced off into a ditch.
It was the Aryan races again, proving their superiority,
As if anyone could possibly doubt it.
– It is enough to make one sicken of the human project,
Its towns, its pick-up trucks, its ever-extending and branching
        tree of mendacious conceptions –
And for a moment even the streets of Birmingham
Seemed populated by demons.

9.

You respect what resists your will, said Immanuel Kant.
That is why the unhappy tyrant respects nothing
Save his own astounding caprices.
And Freud said the luckless ego
Is slave to three masters –
He must have been forgetting Birmingham,
Thinking of the id and the superego.

10.

This message spoken in the Jurassic
Comes to me without the smallest distortion –
I stand stroking the fine spokes of a gingko leaf
In Birmingham's Botanical Gardens.

11.

That summer evening in Birmingham
– Street sweet with the scent of heliotrope –
Thousands of ants were milling about on the sidewalk.
Many were winged, some went naked,
All were in ardent confusion.
And I remembered my teenage excitement, realising
That every girl in the city
Had two breasts and a vagina.

12.

I once walked around central Birmingham
With a handsome young soldier
Who wanted to show me how to pick up girls.
His enthusiastic "Well, *hullo* there!" certainly created a sensation
On several occasions
But it can't I think have achieved the desired effect
For we both returned home to his wife at the close of the evening.

13.

When Robert Frost had finished praising New Hampshire
He wrote: "At present, I am living in Vermont".
That is the nature of praise,
We use it to love what is absent.
That is why we praise God with such fervour
And the abiding city.
And perhaps if I lived in Birmingham
I should be writing poems in praise of West Hampstead.

MARESTAIL, OR PRIEST'S PRICK

When he was a boy, in the pious village,
The man who could turn dumb bread into living flesh
Was a magician! You could forget driving tractors
Or milking cows, those rather mucky activities –
The man in the black dress, with the plump hands
And the lovely, moderate voice, he was the one to resemble!
He clung to his mother. And there was the mysterious celibacy.
That was better as well. It was something to do with soap
And Sunday mornings when he could gorge on the feeling of
    goodness,
Walking toward the tolling bell
In clean clothes, hair burnished, holding the beautiful ruby-red
    prayer-book…

– Later, he realised he had never believed a word of it.
And he enjoyed describing that persistent weed, the marestail,
As priest's prick, always getting in if you don't pay proper
    attention.

THE CHESTNUT TREE

This beautiful chestnut tree
Was cut across at the bole:
Five stems became five tall
Trunks in a tall bouquet,
Like a five-branched candlestick
Flourished against the sky.
He thinks, as he saunters by:
"Nothing has held the tree back
From beauty and forceful growth,
Despite that sickening cut
Which broke it early in youth,
And caused it to deviate
From all it might have been,
From all it could have foreseen."

PREGNANT WOMAN

Water stained brown with peat and strung with chains
Of foam from the tumultuous falls behind her;
Beeches in autumn glory all around her;
The tawny lichens where the warmth remains –

She came here day by day to sit and dream,
The more intently for her ignorance
Of whether fortune, or unfortunate mischance,
Drew her thus from her home to seek the stream.

About her a strange joy began to hover.
Father long lost, between husband and lover –
The sunlight seemed to toy with shape, and gather:

As if all-loving God, by special favour,
Had called her by his grace, which faileth never,
To bear this child and not know the father.

SOME PEOPLE JUST AREN'T RELIABLE

Now they were nowhere to be seen. The day
Became oppressive. Trees reached silently
Against the light-filled, unapproachable sky.
The glossy pool lay *shtum*, and would not play.

What had come over the sun he could not judge.
The petunias' puce had never seemed so hot.
A fly whined its unique and languid note.
Time which speeds by stood fast and would not budge.

Then they came back. They were subdued and kind,
As if to assure him he was in their mind
In that weird interval when the world was static.

And time started again. Trees became normal,
Flies buzzed as usual. But they still seemed formal –
Almost, he thought, they seemed apologetic.

DESIRES
after Cavafy

They are like beautiful bodies that age has not touched
And that you lay gently with tears in a magnificent tomb
With roses at their head and, at their feet, jasmine –
They are like such bodies, these desires which now are quenched
Without ever having asserted themselves, without ever having
                              were it but one
Single night of pleasure or one enchanted dawn.

I HEAR IT SAID OF DANTE

I hear it said of Dante that by Beatrice
He spoke of Christ. What anger and what grief
Ties up my heart. It is on your account,
Katya, I am so angry, for I believe
I have no reason to feel envy of others,
Having known you, and in your youth and mine.
And yet I let you pass. I knew, and yet
Could not believe, I had such little faith,
That you were Christ-like, that, after twenty years,
I could still be holding girls in conversation
Because their laughing smile, or high cheekbones,
Remind me of you. Now
I need to rid myself of that delusion,
Well-known to bleeding lovers, that all who remain
Are all the same, all other-than-Katya,
And have no merit except by seeming like her.
I who supposed my life was armour-plated
Against despair by premature non-attachment
Stand blinking mooncalf-like in normal daylight.
My cynicism was my innocence;
And I must end it painfully, and with
Humiliation, guilt, and such repining
You'd think I'd lost some lovelier maidenhead.

ABSENCE

I weave this web
I undo it in the evening
I weave this web
I undo it in the evening

The rough-voiced suitors drink from the barrels
In the palace of Ithaca
"Real life" goes on in the halls
I weave this web

My heart is not in weaving the web
Yet it is withheld from the suitors
I imagine a man, active and strong, like a dolphin!
I undo it in the evening

I imagine he is swimming to me
But in great circles
Dawn breaks, again the horizon is empty
I weave this web

If I imagine the axe-blades of the Trojans
If I imagine tall younger women, like Goddesses
If I imagine the blind hungry mouths of the sea
I undo it in the evening

The suitors are real men
They have strong legs and loud voices
They can wait, they are amused at my refusals
I weave this web

In the web I have woven a woman
She is standing, no longer young
No longer, as she was, the most rapt of the dancers
I undo it in the evening

If his bow did not stand in the hall
Which no-one else can draw
If his son did not stand in the hall
I should doubt he ever existed

RE-WRITING A POEM

I think I'm rewriting a poem
I wrote five years ago;
In which I rewrote a poem
Written five years before;
In which I rewrote a poem,
Written five years before;
In which –
And so it goes, down the decades
Till I find a desperate baby
Speaking the pristine poem –
Crying: *Turn to me! look at me!*
Love me! weep for me!
O! be moved by my sorrow,
Stone-faced mother of mine!

RILKE
(Poem written when he was dying from leukaemia)

Come you, you last one, whom I now acknowledge,
Unhealable pain in the body's intricate web:
As I burned in the spirit, look! I burn
In you; the wood has so long struggled against
Consenting to the tireless flame you blaze with –
Yet now I nourish you, and burn in you.
My mild, this-worldly being turns in your fury
Into a Fury from Hell and not from here.
Quite pure, quite plan-less, free of futures I
Climbed on this dizzy pyre of suffering,
So sure of nowhere buying in a future
For this heart whose supplies have all gone silent.
Am I still it, burning unrecognisably?
I find no memories to drag across.
O life! life! To be outside of it.
And I in flame. Nobody who knows me.

GOETHE
Phenomenon

When with the wall of rain
Bright Phoebus mates,
Brilliant, that bow again
Heaven creates.

I see the same arc show
In white mist drawn:
White, but yet still that bow,
Still heaven-born.

Old man, you may still be
Joyful enough.
White though your hair may be,
Yet you will love.

III

The toil of love

Thrawn cattle are thae words
coost up at me by thocht
at inconvenient times,
raither fand nor socht –

ROBERT GARIOCH

… Nor had I time to Love –
But since
Some Industry must be –
The little Toil of Love –
I thought
Be large enough for Me –

EMILY DICKINSON

After sixty years my gums are not so good.
I dental-floss them in the one-sex toilet.
Returning, clamber over wife and daughter
And look down five miles to the Hindu Kush.
You can see how India butts into Eurasia:
Flat plates and frills of mountain rear and crumble
Far as the eye sees through this luminous ocean
On which our plane is riding, almost motionless,
Almost without a tremble, as it eats
The flavourless kilometres. In front of me,
A computer geek in glasses has kept closed
His blind since Kuala Lumpur. On the monitors
The arrows marking Mecca have rotated
To almost along the wing. Two countries away
Across this lion-coloured world a war
Is brewing. I imagine
Our air-conditioned bubble dropping bombs
On the tiny square of village far below me,
Less than a camel's footprint. I get dizzy,
Peering directly down. No bombs are dropped.
Nor would they be if I were captain here
Over this fragile, integrated planet,
Spinning unscripted. Our bubble carries us,
Deep in computer solitaire or sleeping –
Safe, I can hardly say that, but for this moment
Warm in the thin air and the killing cold.

THE COLOUR YELLOW

I

There is no colour I want to see except these yellow tulips!
They make even the daffodils I love look lemony and diluted.
Their yellow does not remind me of anything: commanding eyes,
    yielding breasts –
is neither severe nor enchanting – it does not recall
Beethoven's Fourth piano concerto, or dawn in the vast sky
    above the bay at St. Andrews,
or London's cherry-blossom in sunshine between April
    showers –
This yellow is dense, unutterable, clearly objective, clean of all
    meanings,
varies only because of the sunlight and the overlapping of petals.
I feed on it and feed on it with an insatiable appetite,
fuelling an unknown metabolism.

II

Happy toad, said Max Jacob.
You don't have to wear a yellow star

I knew a painter who could never think of yellow
without remembering the yellow star
he had to wear in his boyhood.
For him it rang false like the cracked
bell of a leper

58

An old soldier said to me, in passionate self-disgust,
he had a streak of yellow
right up his back!

I once heard that the King of Denmark,
filled with contempt for his Nazi occupiers,
bicycled around Copenhagen
wearing a yellow star

III

Yet when June, who was named for summer,
told me yellow was her favourite colour,
I was taken aback –
I had never even considered it! –
as if red, green, blue
were the only colours that could carry such weight.
Now, as in so many things,
I agree with her.

REFLECTIONS ON THE EVE OF THE IRAQ WAR

I

Full moon distracts me to my office window:
Small glittering disc climbing the night-black sky,
Framed in her mist of radiance. I
Put her at once in role: the point of reference
From which the hubbub of our history can
Be reconfigured; that parent in the North
To whom the son repairs for consultation,
Penitence, and advice. The world is changing
In ways beyond our imagery; we are becoming
Something we can't conceive of nor transcend,
And must submit to. It is a dying –
The all-too-obvious night-time metaphor
That round the curve of planet Earth explodes
In building-shattering fact. But here, at 8 o'clock
In privileged England I need not fear
The guns, the stumbling tanks, B52s,
The F16s and Harriers freighted down
Like murderous insects with their ordnance; can only
Sense the rending
Of our collective fabric, and half-whimsically
Speak my despair to this hard glittering disc.

My father lives next door and he is dying.
No matter how loud the racket in my house
I am listening for him, sensitive to even
The softest crashes.
My father lives next door and he is dying.

My father lives next door; he does not know me.
Old warrior, whiteish, toothless, groping terrified
From sink to chair, from chair to lavatory,
I grieve your fierceness.
My father lives next door; he does not know me.

My father lives next door; his eyes are inward.
What does he see? I think his eyes are blind.
What do you see, Father? He does not answer.
His words are over.
My father lives next door; his words are over.

III

God will not come out of the house at evening
And call *OK, you rowdy children! supper!*
And those who die because of these bombardments
Are someone's mother, someone's son or sister.
The smoke and lies of war blacken the earth
Again, huge guns recoil, bombs
Hurtle like rats, and where there was clean water
Or careful craftsmanship, now is dust and ruin.
Morality is conjured, tossed, and trashed.

Out of the past a soft voice whispering:
How with this rage can beauty hold a plea?
Whose action...

Perhaps there is nothing good but conversation
With what we love, and tragedy
Is when one is denied it. That truthful face,
Talking without reserve, taking for granted
That you will fathom all the depths and heights
Of her communication, touches something
And knits together something steeply different
From these blood-drenched exchanges. *Pray to survive,*
I tell her, *pray to survive undamaged*
And feed our children with such conversation.

I think Elytis put it well:
He said, *Build, brothers! build a fountain!*
He meant, ignore the pomp and uproar.
Build what will give refreshment
And graceful motion to a cherished future.

THE SUNLIT SURFACES

Ein Bild des Glaubens ist die schöne Weib:
Sie ist ein ja, und sie ist grenzenlos.
– F. Schuon

The summer sun brings tables out on the sidewalks.
At the age of 60, sitting in a café,
He becomes conscious again how someone's knee
– The conniving perpendiculars of thigh and shin,
The complex full and hollows of the kneebone –
Compels desire, and with desire, longing.
(Desire is by its nature ever-new,
Drives to self-quenching action, whereas longing
Strives without wanting, is the blaze itself.)
His gaze returns, and nothing else intrigues it.
A woman's body wakens consciousness
So intense it leads to stupor unless managed,
Held back by fire-breaks or, by a barrel, aimed
At some particular target. How one longs
To die, to drown, in those ogival planes!

Formerly, of course, it was unbalancing glimpses,
Rapunzel's mighty hair, the arms of mermaids,
Where matter seemed to blur its self-containment.
The elaborate ship, that slipped its moorings, vanished
At once in fog, left only churning water
To slap and splash under a midnight wharf.
Later, the fog had lifted, but the ship
Now seemed prosaic, seemed like a rowing-boat
Oared clumsily by children, going in circles;
And then – sea-bells! the lovely bunting fluttered,

The raffia streamers could no longer hold the
Moving liner. Small tugs drew out ahead,
With rigid cables over their shoulders.

                          All that
Carried the charm of novelty, gone now
Yet never quite supplanted: mind knows the truth but stays
A happy victim: summer after summer
The ordinary chaos of the body,
Combed and combined and primed for provocation,
Emerges like artillery onto the street
And guns him down like Tammuz, laughing
As he is dismembered. You'd wish for him,
If he had his life again, that someone would
Warn him effectively about July.

Yet maybe you'd be wrong. The thoughts of sex,
Those hilarious putti carrying Mars's helmet
Which leave nobility naked, draw us toward
The proximate flesh, the face, the watchful eyes
We had forgotten at our grown-up distance.
Body is known – we don't struggle to recall it,
Although we had forgotten –
Is known so strangely that its closeness speaks
With a sudden shock the only human language
In the gross backdrop of inhuman hubbub.
In which propinquity (O Margarethe!
O Shulamith!),
You are named uniquely, thought sweetens and divines

What poets meant by those insistent potencies –
Penelope, Mary, *das Ewig-Weibliche,*
The child whom boyish Dante loved, and found
His guide to Heaven when he got there finally:
Which image, deeply established, changes everything,
Clouds, winds and ocean into breath and blood.

Now in this café in the silencing sunlight,
Aware of youthful flesh, he has awakened
From the stark surfaces of knives and buildings,
Figures in matter which he may acknowledge
But which won't answer him. Conceive that racing ship
Over the dazzling ocean where Isolde
Sleeps in the prow. Both she and you have drunk
The potion, and your destinies are fixed
Now, regardless of physics. Heart-mysteries there,
As Yeats might say, yet all still held in matter,
The stuff of which you are made. Your thoughts are free
To go apart, yet all your freedom
You will spend in re-uniting. Here then is the god Amor
Whose inner name is *Joy,* whose viewless force,
Like the swimmer crashing down through emerald water,
Discovers to you void, astounding depths
– How suddenly entered! like happening on a secret –
No way conflicting with the sunlit surface.

LINDISFARNE: THE RUINED PRIORY IN SUNLIGHT

High tide converts this spit of dunes to island,
And here the Celtic Christians built their chapel
To pray among the pagan Anglo-Saxons.
– But the summer sun banishes interest
In vanished histories of woe and piety!
The extravagant butterflies probe the purple buddleias,
And my thoughts repeat a quotation from Confucius:
"How am I fallen from myself! For a long time now
I have not seen the Prince of Chang in my dreams."

And last night I re-met you, Katya. Tall and naked,
You stood in a cabin, perhaps a changing-room,
Undimmed by the years that have dethroned the rest of us.
I was as always unsurprised to see you.
We talked as friends, and I was somewhere timid
Because of your perfection and held back
From sexual contact or (perhaps I feared)
Some clumsy act of speechless adoration. Even so,
I knew by your presence, by your body
My question about the worth of human life,
My lurking disparagement of this incarnation,
Was starkly dispelled, became unfindable.
You are like I think some store of excellence
Which stretches out to the remotest stars
To dab them with your colour; or like a boat
Which, when the sheets pull, gives the whole ocean meaning.

Is it a mystery or a simple fact
That your beauty shaped my history – that since that morning

When we met so easily in the green Aegean
(Not all that far from Cyprus!), I have known you, loved you,
Dreamed of you and in your sunlight altered every component
That makes my daily life, my friends, my work?
You are what Confucius meant by the Prince of Chang.
You are both simple fact and mystery,
And no more need explaining than the sun,
Giver of life to all life's feeding kingdoms,
Owes to the ardent peacock butterflies
An explanation of the buddleia.

ST. JOHN ON PATMOS

After the nightmare, after the lucubrations
And crashing on the brain's organ until you feared
It would break with such a weight of music –

                        where is there left to go
But downward, into the peace of rock and sand
And brackish water lolling among the shingle?
Angels are not delusion but their presence fades.
How still the world is when the mind is silent!
You love the fresh calling of the oyster-catchers
Across the bay. You are ageless now,
Gaunt awkward angular man, unoccupied,
And surprisingly healthy considering what you have come through.
Those Whores and horses, the Virgin and her moon,
The moral fury –
The sky-wide banners and the all-dominant trumpets
No longer detain your attention. They resemble
Dissolving flags that transiently stain
The slates and blues of dawn. Now they are gone.
The clear cool lovely colours take you by the hand.

And now your other life begins – or not begins,
But is foregrounded, is the life you will live
Until your death, which is a part of it.
Strange how there's nothing unfamiliar
About this freedom, as if you always knew
It was waiting for you, unperemptorily,
Like a glass of water after a drunken party,
Reconstituting pleasure. Now, everything
Is what it seems, and so it always was

You can't help thinking, ironic among your rocks.
(Irony also is a luxury
Not worth retaining.) So it always was.
You watch a sea-bird with unshuddering wings
Glide sheerly from the cliff-face and sweep upward,
Pause, and continue on a perfect gradient
Never before travelled, on dependable air.
Life need not continue and it need not stop.
You see (or I the poet see on your behalf)
No God requires your bent spine or your prayers.
And no Apocalypse will be more real
Than these washing waves, this water, and these stones.

CHRISTIAN THEOLOGY

The fly that has to negotiate this orchid
Is weary with the complication of the trumpet,
The baroque pistils, the astounding stamens,
– But reaches, finally, the drop of nectar...

GAUTAMA: THOUGHTS IN SAVERNAKE FOREST

It was not an accident that Gautama sat
In the forest beneath a peepul tree
And saw all things were connected, all things rose
From the past's black water where the eye grows giddy.
If he were with me, seated on this log,
I would show him how this floor of fallen oak-leaves,
So dry and papery on its topmost surface,
Is made geometrical by small acorn-cups
And broken bracken-stems, each one of which
Is mottled and dashed with short straight streaks, like hyphens –
And how, beneath these surface leaves
Are other leaves, darker, and damp, decaying,
Disintegrating, turning back to earth,
Retaining the shape of oak-leaves as they lose
Shape altogether. And I would show him
(As if he needed showing!) how this beech-tree
Offers against the sky's blank blue its springing
Antlers of tiny leaf-buds, each one tremulous
As if on the delicatest Alexander Calder stabile,
Yet proffered merely by any branch of a beech-tree;
And I would show him –

But then, dear Gautama, then I would remember
That you've met these things already, that your joy
And clear contemplative spirit fill the forest
Because I look at it, knowing your thought,
Conveyed to me through trillions of transmissions, each unique
And subtle with an intricacy past conceiving.

– Yet though, like you, I know I cannot fall
Out of connectedness, I am alone
Here in the forest, as you too were alone
That dawn when, disentangling yourself, you stepped
Out from beneath your peepul tree and recognised
You had now found all you had sought! – O, light in the sky!
O, breathing forest! – and there, confronting you,
Stood the God Brahma, God of all first creations
– You had seen through gods, of course, and knew their origin –
With whom you argued but did not insist
When he told you to return to Varanasi.

For, to be truthful, you who loved all beings,
You who had lost your mother, and who had abandoned
Wife and child in that lust for contemplation –
You longed to be back in the world of men.

LEGEND

His voice was beautiful; his eyes were shining;
His song rose peerless from the forest floor.
From buttresses to soaring battlements
Song shaped the air as never song before.

He sang her courage and he sang her kindness,
Sang how her beauty sprang from both of these.
Joy that she *was* saluted her each morning,
Rose like an exhalation from the trees.

And she was stirred. From her high battlements
She gave instruction: bring that man to me.
Bring me the singer of that peerless love-song
And we shall love in song and symphony.

They brought him in. He was a broad-backed peasant,
A Harlequin who'd dreamed himself Pierrot.
She squinted down the stair, then told a servant
To give him porridge and get him to go.

GOLDEN WEDDING

Age had not altered his authority
But made him playful to his guests' approaches.
Laughter and silver hair and glinting brooches
Lit up his progress through the big marquee.

One image came as it had often done,
No way disturbing his dispensing pleasure:
Wrecked sheets beneath a thrown-wide window; the pressure
Of a girl astride him, arched in sunlit dawn.

Proud as he was of fifty years of marriage,
And careful certainly not to disparage
The spouse who shared his tall posterity,

He could not quite wish that the thought would perish
Which shone within him – caused him still to cherish,
Bright down decades, one brief adultery.

TWO AT A PARTY

Cupid has lit the love-lights in her eyes,
And here she is again, at sixty plus,
Gazing (responsible, and rapturous)
At her old colleague, who still can magnetize

– Despite cancer, retirement, and white hair –
Her poised rejoinders and hilarious sparring.
He too is magnetized: witty, co-starring,
He rules the truths of history from his chair.

And what's in this for me? Am I still youthful,
Projecting from youth's eminence my truthful,
Affectionate-satirical erotic arrows?

No, on the contrary: I am like her,
Entranced that his courageous joy and flair
Still keeps the world great as the future narrows.

MEDITATION ON A LINE OF SHAKESPEARE (SONNET 31)

"Thou art the grave where buried love doth live" –
And as I love you all my loves revive.
You needn't be jealous that they're still alive:
Their life in me is your unconscious gift.

You remember that rope of firecrackers, high as the house,
We saw in Amsterdam? and as the blaze
Sank fussing down the clay-red cartridges,
Detonation after detonation blasted us!

The confusing years I am tempted to regret
(And neither well remember, nor forget)
Are unexpectedly re-shaped and ranked

And what seemed meaningless, or was left broken,
Or stayed opaque, obscure, can now stand simply open –
Sunlit and flawed in this Spring warmth of thanks.

IN MEMORY OF PIPPIN
1991-2007

Alert small bitch, half-terrier,
Half-whippet, with the strength and speed
Bestowed by each parental breed –
You reach the close of your career.

So long the path down which you've fared,
Memory is hard-pressed to recall
The hurtling canine cannonball
Who'd greet us when we hardly dared

Open the front-door, and who'd then
Rush off and rip her blanket up
To celebrate. On a cliff-top
Or open field you'd find again

Your racing forebears and for hours
Go like the wind. Equally true
That you could lie the whole day through
Quiet in your basket. Disliking showers

And terrified by fireworks: we
Deployed our cleverest arts to guess
What traumas you could not express
Brought you, homeless, to Battersea

Where you squeaked, fearing to be spurned –
And were so timid when selected
That when rebuked you went dejected
To the front gate to be returned.

– Well, Pippin with the questioning ears
That scanned like radar, always cocked,
The slender forepaws which you crossed
Neatly at the wrists, for fifteen years

You were not rejected. Now, gone deaf,
Incontinent, face ash-white, not brown:
We've called the vet to put you down.
Shocked by our power to end your life,

These breaking tears put us in touch
With both our loves: for you, and this
Our dubious breed whose gift it is
To care so cruelly, and so much.

THE DOUBLE BASS

In life I did much good; I chaired Ethical Committees and sat on
　　the Board of the National Lottery, and I was declared a
　　benefactor of the human race.

As a reward I have been reincarnated as a double bass.

It was my choice. The archangel Gabriel offered me numerous
　　possibilities. "Gods?" he said: "demons? Jenghiz Khan?
　　Marilyn Monroe?

Lion? Dolphin? Lake Baikal? Suilven? a big star? a little minnow?"

"Thank you," I said politely, "thank you, but no,"

(for I am one who remembers his place),

"having fulfilled all my ambit-

ions, I am left with just one wish,

and that is, to be a double bass."

This was no problem to the archangel Gabriel. "A first double bass?"
　　he said, "or one a bit secondary?"

"Definitely a first," I said, "if it's up to me."

"Done!" he said. "Done!" I said. He said, "Done again!"

And thus the thing was effected. It was not a Faustian bargain.

For now I have fulfilled my final wish, and I am ready to step
down from the wheel of death and rebirth.

I have carried in *basso profondo* ripples the melody of Beethoven's
Ninth Symphony, and I have made my last demand on the
earth.

p. 16 'Apus apus': Latin name for the swift. (*Apus* = footless.)

p. 35 'Two Shots at an Elegy': Peter Caddy was co-founder with his wife Eileen of the Findhorn Foundation, an ecologically-minded New Age community by the Moray Firth. "In perfect timing" was a favourite phrase in many of his stories, and became the title of his autobiography.

p. 47 'Desires' (after Cavafy): I have translated Cavafy's poem from the French translation by Gilles Ortlieb and Pierre Leyris.

p. 52 'Rilke: Poem written when he was dying from Leukaemia': Rilke wrote this poem in 1926, a few days before his death. The leukaemia that killed him had been stalking him for about four years. Perhaps not a great poem but one showing exceptional courage.

p. 57 'January 2003': The date is two months before American and British forces invaded Iraq.

p. 58 'The Colour Yellow': Lest anyone take at face-value the self-disgust of an old soldier, I wrote a brief parenthesis describing him. I took it out because it spoiled the balance of the poem, but to do him justice it should be included. It went:

> *(He had crossed a dangerous road*
> *to reconnoitre,*
> *leaving his platoon in a ditch.*
> *Every last one of them*
> *died under mortar-fire)*

p. 64 'The Sunlit Surfaces': The epigraph translates: "A beautiful woman is the image of faith. She is a yes, and she is without limit." In the body of the poem, *das Ewig-Weibliche* (Goethe's phrase) translates literally as "the Eternal-Womanly"; its meaning probably can't be said, quite, in contemporary English.

p. 69 'St. John on Patmos': Not the gospel-writer but the author of the last book of the Bible, the Apocalypse (Book of Revelation). I have followed the example of many painters in relocating "Patmos" to an island more familiar to me, in this case Tanera Mor in the Summer Isles.

p. 72 'Gautama: Thoughts in Savernake Forest': The accent in Gautama falls on the first syllable.

D. M. Black is a Scottish poet, born in South Africa in 1941, brought up in Scotland from 1950. He now lives in London and Wiltshire. In 1991 he produced a *Collected Poems* (Polygon), having previously published four collections of poems and a number of pamphlets. He was included in the first series of Penguin Modern Poets (no. 11, 1968) and his poems have appeared in many anthologies including: *British Poetry since 1945* (Penguin, 1970), edited by Edward Lucie-Smith; *The Faber Book of Twentieth Century Scottish Poetry* (Faber, 1992), edited by Douglas Dunn; *Emergency Kit* (Faber, 1996), edited by Jo Shapcott and Matthew Sweeney; *Generations* (Penguin, 1998), edited by Melanie Hart and James Loader; *A Quark for Mr. Mark: 101 Poems about Science* (Faber, 2000), edited by Maruice Riordan and Jon Turney; *Apollinaire* (Everyman, 2000), edited by Robert Chandler; and *Wild Reckoning* (Calouste Gulbenkian Foundation, 2004), edited by Maurice Riordan and John Burnside. Since 1991 he has published a collection of translations of Goethe, *Love as Landscape Painter*, and individual poems in a variety of journals including *Modern Poetry in Translation*, *Poetry London*, *Stand*, *Thumbscrew* and the *TLS*.

Recent titles in Arc Publications'
POETRY FROM THE UK / IRELAND,
include:

LIZ ALMOND
The Shut Drawer
Yelp!

JAMES BYRNE
Blood / Sugar

JONATHAN ASSER
Outside The All Stars

DONALD ATKINSON
In Waterlight: Poems New,
Selected & Revised

ELIZABETH BARRETT
A Dart of Green & Blue

JOANNA BOULTER
Twenty Four Preludes & Fugues on
Dmitri Shostakovich

THOMAS A CLARK
The Path to the Sea

TONY CURTIS
What Darkness Covers
The Well in the Rain

JULIA DARLING
Sudden Collapses in Public Places
Apology for Absence

CHRIS EMERY
Radio Nostalgia

LINDA FRANCE
You are Her

KATHERINE GALLAGHER
Circus-Apprentice
Carnival Edge

CHRISSIE GITTINS
Armature

RICHARD GWYN
Sad Giraffe Café

MICHAEL HASLAM
The Music Laid Her Songs in Language
A Sinner Saved by Grace
A Cure for Woodness

MICHAEL HULSE
The Secret History

BRIAN JOHNSTONE
The Book of Belongings

JOEL LANE
Trouble in the Heartland
The Autumn Myth

HERBERT LOMAS
The Vale of Todmorden
A Casual Knack of Living
(COLLECTED POEMS)

PETE MORGAN
August Light

MICHAEL O'NEILL
Wheel

MARY O'DONNELL
The Ark Builders

IAN POPLE
An Occasional Lean-to

PAUL STUBBS
The Icon Maker

SUBHADASSI
peeled

LORNA THORPE
A Ghost in My House

MICHELENE WANDOR
Musica Transalpina
Music of the Prophets

JACKIE WILLS
Fever Tree
Commandments